Our Family Prayer Book

Our Family Prayer Book

✠

Renee Bartkowski

LIGUORI
PUBLICATIONS

One Liguori Drive
Liguori, MO 63057-9999
(314) 464-2500

ISBN 0-89243-628-X
Library of Congress Catalog Card Number: 94-75244

Cover design by Pam Hummelsheim

Table of Contents

I
Our Home and Family

✠

Our Home 15

Our Family 16

Our Bond 17

Our Peace 18

II
Living With Ourselves

✠

Self-Worth 21

Growing Up 22

Personal Responsibility 23

Concern for Others 24

Talents 25

III

Our Relationship With God

✠

Faith 29

Prayer 30

Church 31

God's Presence 32

God's Invitation 33

Silence 34

IV

Facing Life

✠

Happiness 37

Humor 38

The Good and the Bad 39

Change 40

Simplicity 41

Priorities 42

V

Our Relationship With One Another

✠

Acceptance 45

Sensitivity..................................... 46

Frustrations 47

Talking and Listening 48

Being Pleasant............................. 49

Disagreements 50

Apologies and Forgiveness 51

VI

Daily Responsibilities

✠

Cooperation 55

Chores 56

Finances 57

Rules 58

VII

Learning How to Live

✠

Failure 61

Helpfulness 62

A Positive Attitude 63

Openness 64

Criticism 65

Compromise 66

Convictions 67

VIII

Living With Our Feelings

✠

Moodiness 71

Fear 72

Self-Pity 73

Anger 74

Contentment 75

IX
Coping With Our Faults

Jealousy 79
Selfishness 80
Honesty 81
Pride 82
Worry 83
Complaints 84

X
Living With Others

Love 87
Prejudice 88
Gossip 89
Blessings 90
Neighborliness 91
Friendliness 92

XI

Today's Problems and Standards

✠

Values 95

Alcohol 96

Drugs 97

Sex 98

Peer Pressure 99

Authority 100

XII

Our Goals and Achievements

✠

Mission 103

Effort 104

Competition 105

Challenge and Opportunity 106

Hopes and Dreams 107

XIII
Prayers for Special Needs

✠

A Problem 111

An Illness 112

Sadness and Grief 113

A Difficult Time 114

An Important Decision 115

When We Travel 116

XIV
Special Times

✠

Our Family's Birthday 119

A Birthday 120

Easter 121

Thanksgiving 122

Christmas 123

Achievement 124

A Special Guest 125

The Great Outdoors 126

Reunions 127

I

Our
Home
and
Family

Our Home

We ask you, Lord, to bless our home.
We invite you to come and live with us
in this precious dwelling of ours
and to help us make it into a special place
that's filled with your love and your peace.
Dear God, let our home
be a place that will always provide us
with safety and security;
a place where we can always find
strength, understanding, and support;
a place where we can always help one another
grow in your love.
Teach us, Lord, how to make our home
into a haven of comfort and companionship,
into a sanctuary where we can always find someone
with whom we can share our concerns,
with whom we can laugh and cry—
someone who will give us a hug
when we need one.
Help us, Lord, to make our home
into a warm and inviting shelter
where we can give our love and companionship
to friends, relatives, and neighbors,
to those who are lonely and need
our welcoming arms.
Bless all people, Lord, who do not live
in comfortable homes.

Amen ✠

Our Family

Lord, let us always be aware of how lucky we are
   to be part of a loving and caring family.
   There are times when we disagree with one another—
      and argue and tease others.
There are times
   when we're a real pain in the neck to one another.
But in spite of all this,
   we really do care about one another, Lord,
      and we always try to be there for one another.
When any of us are struggling
   with problems and fears,
      our family is there to give us
      the love and support we need.
When we're forced to cope with disappointment
      or failure,
   our family is there to encourage us and
      cheer us on.
They may get annoyed with us at times,
   but they don't stop loving us—
      even when we're sulky and crabby
      and not easy to live with.
They may complain, but in the end,
      they put up with our moodiness
         and forgive us for our bad behavior.
Where else can we find people
   who are so loyal and accepting?
We thank you, Lord, for giving us the chance
   to be part of this family.

Amen ✠

Our Bond

Lord, help us to remain a close-knit, loving, caring group.
    Don't let us become the type of family
        that drifts apart and loses interest in one another.
    There are so many things that take up our time
        and pull us away from one another—
            our activities at school and church,
            our involvement in sports,
            working long hours at our jobs,
            spending time with our friends.
        Some days, we don't even get to eat dinner together.
Help us, Lord, achieve balance in our lives.
    Let us be willing to make time for one another—
        to listen to one another's problems,
        to share one another's interests,
        to express our pride in one another's achievements,
        to enjoy one another's companionship.
When we feel that we're drifting apart, Lord,
    let us go out of our way
        to plan something special together—
            perhaps a special dinner or picnic,
            an occasional family game night,
            a relaxing "TV and popcorn evening" at home.
    Help us to always remain close to one another
        so that when we leave home
            to live our own lives,
        we will remain available to help,
            to care, and to lend the support that is needed.
We thank you, Lord, for all the love and friendship
    we share as a family.

Amen ✤

Our Peace

Lord, so many families experience strained relationships,
    envy, and resentment.
  We know of families
    in which parents argue,
    brothers fight,
    sisters do not speak to one another.
  We know of families
    that know no sense of loyalty, unity, or respect.
Lord, bless and help those families
    that are torn apart by dissension and abuse.
  Help those families that experience separation
    because they find it impossible to love
      and live together peacefully.
Dear Lord, protect our family from ever experiencing
    the strain of hatred and envy and lack of love.
  We ask you to help each of us
    to develop the ability to get along with one another,
    to pull together and work together,
    to love, support, and respect one another.
Let us realize, Lord, that if we want a home
  that's peaceful and enjoyable to live in,
    it's the responsibility of each of us
      to do our part in making our home
      peaceful and enjoyable.
Let each of us willingly accept this responsibility
  by always going out of our way
    to be pleasant, forgiving, and kind.

Amen ✠

II

Living
With
Ourselves

Self-Worth

Lord, there are times when we feel like such blobs.
  We feel clumsy and unimportant and inadequate.
Help each of us, Lord, to feel good about ourselves.
    Teach us to recognize and appreciate our assets
            and talents
        and to avoid letting ourselves become discouraged
            by our weaknesses and limitations.
  Let us realize that—because we are human—
      we are not perfect,
      we all have faults,
      we all make mistakes,
      we all do foolish and embarrassing things.
  Let us learn how to forgive ourselves
      for our mistakes and our weaknesses.
  Let us learn to spend more time
      doing the best we can with what we have
          and less time worrying
              about what we can't do or don't have.
When we find it hard to have faith in ourselves, Lord,
  let us know and feel that you have faith in us.
We ask you, Lord, not only to love us
  when we find it difficult to love ourselves,
      but to teach us how to view and value ourselves
          as the unique, precious individuals we are.
  Let us learn to feel secure in your sight.
  Let us learn to feel joy
      in knowing that you care about every one of us,
      that you love us just as we are.

Amen ✠

Growing Up

At times, Lord, we act like children—
    we sulk and pout and want our own way,
    we demand and let our tempers flare.
Lord, help us all to grow up,
    to leave our childish ways behind,
    to become more mature,
        more responsible, and more pleasant.
    Help us develop patience
        so we can treat one another
            with kindness and forgiveness.
    Help us develop understanding
        so we can accept one another as we are.
    Help us develop honesty
        so we can be trusted in everything we do.
    Help us develop a sense of responsibility
        so that it's unnecessary for us
            to be constantly pushed and prodded
                to do the things we must,
                    for the good of the family.
Teach us, dear Lord,
    to control our tempers,
    to be ready and willing to compromise,
    and to be willing to go out of our way
        to keep our relationships with others
            peaceful and pleasant.
    Teach us how to face life
        with a more positive, contented, and mature outlook.
Lord, let us grow and develop into the kind of people
    that you want us to be.

Amen ✠

Personal Responsibility

Lord, sometimes we are tempted to blame others
    for what we are.
Let us always remember
    that we become what we want to become.
    No one can force us to be what we don't want to be,
        and no one can influence us
            unless we choose to be influenced.
    Sometimes we fool ourselves into thinking that
        when we do something wrong,
            it isn't really our fault;
            it's somebody else's fault;
            it's the fault of some injustice;
            it's the fault of society in general.
But that isn't true, is it, Lord?
    When we're tempted to blame,
        remind us that you created us
            with a will that is free—
                free to choose good or bad,
                free to choose kindness or meanness,
                free to choose love and understanding
                    or anger and resentment,
                free to choose to work on our faults
                    or to stubbornly hold on to them.
Let us always remember, Lord,
    to use the freedom you have given us
        to develop ourselves
            into good, likable, and responsible people.

Amen ✠

Concern for Others

Lord, teach us to think of others first.
> It's so easy to be concerned with only ourselves
>> and our own personal problems and interests.
> At times, we become so wrapped up in ourselves
>> that we act as if the whole world revolves around us;
>>> we don't even notice the needs of others.
> There are times when others are hurting or worried,
>> and we're just not aware enough to see it.
>> We're not sensitive enough to even think
>>> of offering help and support.
> Let us realize that people who think only
>> of themselves
>> are usually people who are narrow-minded,
>>> selfish,
>>> even boring.

Remind us, Lord, that we each have the ability—
> and the responsibility—
>> to give of ourselves to others,
>> to give understanding and support to our family,
>> to give help and friendship to our neighbors,
>> to give compassion and encouragement
>>> to those who are suffering and discouraged,
>> to give aid and service
>>> to those who are less fortunate than we are.

Let us always remember, Lord,
> that if we spend more time being concerned
>> about others,
>>> we'll have less time to worry about ourselves.

Amen ✠

Talents

Lord, there are times when we feel that we have no talents.
We often think that only successful people have talent.
We forget that talent includes any ability we might have
that can help enrich our lives and the lives of others.
We all have the talent to be a friend,
to give others our time, attention, help, and support,
to listen, comfort, hug, and love.
Each of us has some abilities—some talents—
with which we can eventually make someone,
somewhere, sometime, a little happier.
Each of us has some abilities—some talents—
with which we can some day, in some way,
make this world a little bit better.
Show each of us, Lord, just where our talents lie,
and help us develop them to the best of our ability.
Let us remember that our talents do not come to us
fully matured and developed.
Let us realize that it takes a lot of effort on our part—
a lot of hard, often tedious, work—
to develop the gifts you have given us.
Help us to stand firm when we are tempted
to be lazy,
to take the easy way out,
to be jealous of or intimidated by
the talents of others.
Let us learn to feel good about the abilities we possess,
to be willing and eager to use them
to make a difference in this small corner
of our world.

Amen ✠

III

Our
Relationship
With
God

Faith

There are times, Lord, when we make such a mess
of our lives.
We make terrible decisions and stupid mistakes.
We stumble along, relying on our ingenuity
to get us through each day—
and we often fail.
When will we learn, Lord, that we need your daily help
to live wisely and well?
Deep down we know we really can't live without you,
yet we constantly keep on trying.
Let us smarten up and become more aware
of just how much we need you in our lives.
Lord, we join together today to tell you that we no longer
want to live our lives without you.
We know that if we have faith and trust in your help,
we'll be able to handle our problems
with much more ease.
We know that with your love and support,
we'll be able to face life's burdens
with much more courage and confidence.
So take us by the hand and lead us, Lord.
Strengthen us when we're troubled.
Comfort us when we're fearful.
Encourage us when we're discouraged.
Enlighten us when we're confused.
Soothe us when we're hurting.
Be with us when we're lonely.
Cheer us up when we feel sad.
Love us when we feel unloved.

Amen ✠

Prayer

Lord, our prayers often sound like Christmas wishlists:
    we want this, we need that, or make something happen.
    We pray "Thy will be done"—
        and in the next breath,
            we tell you exactly what your will should be.
        We often beg you to answer our prayers,
            but all we ever seem to want
                are the answers that we ourselves
                    have already decided are best for us.
There are times, Lord, when we get upset with you,
    even claim that you don't hear us
        because you don't answer our prayers
            exactly as we want them answered.
Dear God, do you ever get tired of listening
    to our narrow-minded demands?
Forgive us, Lord, for trying to tell you what to do.
    Give us the wisdom we need
        to accept and live with answers
            you wish to send to our prayers.
    Give us humility
        that we may be grateful for your love and care.
    Teach us how to pray for your guidance and support
        instead of constantly praying for things
            that we want.
    Let us realize that you, in your wisdom,
        know what we need better than we do.
    Let us realize that you, in your love,
        will provide us with what is best for us.

Amen ✠

Church

Lord, we are thankful that you have given us
 the opportunity to belong to a church,
  to be part of a faith community.
We admit, however, that there are times
 when we fail in our obligation to be faithful,
  when we just don't feel like going to church
   and taking part in prayer
    with the community.
There are times when we go to services
 and just sit there apathetically and daydream.
 Even when we go to church and worship
  halfheartedly and inattentively—
   or when we fail to get there at all—
    you continue to love us.
We know, Lord,
 that you want us to "keep holy the Sabbath"
 and to join our neighbors in taking part
  in the special banquet that you have provided for us.
Lord, let us learn to really appreciate the gifts and graces
 that you give us at these sacred celebrations
  and to be more grateful for the banquet
   with which you so generously nourish us.
Let us learn how to value those hours of togetherness
 that we share with you,
 with our family,
 and with our faith family.
Help us not only to get more out of each celebration
 but to always be willing and eager
  to put more of ourselves into it.

Amen ✠

God's Presence

We often invite you to share our lives with us, Lord—
    and then we divide our lives
        into separate little chunks of living
        and lock you out.
We have a tendency to isolate the spiritual part of life,
    to keep it entirely separate
        from the more "worldly" aspects of living.
We forget that all of life
    should be more integrated into the spiritual,
        that you are willing to share it all with us.
We, therefore, ask you, Lord, to enter into our lives
    and to live each part of each day with us,
        to be with us at home, at school, at our jobs,
        at the store, at the movies, at the game—
        everywhere.
Watch over and bless us, Lord,
    as we eat and sleep,
    energize us as we do our chores,
    have fun with us in our play and relaxation.
Give us your shoulder to lean on
    when our problems weigh us down too heavily.
Take us by the hand and lead us
    when we're not sure where we're going.
Show us, Lord, how we can make each activity,
    each relationship, each smile, each tear—
    each minute of each day—
    into a prayer that we can offer up to you.
Thank you, Lord, for wanting to live
    every part of our lives with us.

Amen ✠

God's Invitation

We feel so much better when we talk to you, Lord,
  when we share our feelings, concerns,
    and problems with you.
  And yet there are times when we actually forget to pray,
    when we turn our backs to you,
    when we ignore your invitation to come to you.
Forgive us, Lord, for all the times
    we have failed to speak to you.
  Forgive us for the times we've ignored your invitation.
  We often wonder how our friends would treat us
    if we treated them as carelessly
      as we sometimes treat you.
        They'd probably eventually turn away from us
          and ignore us too.
But you never do that, Lord.
  You're always near
    inviting us
      and waiting for us to respond.
      And when we finally do,
        you're there,
          holding out your hand to us and saying:
            "Come to me. I'm here for you.
            I'm ready to comfort and help you."
  We are so blessed to have you ever at our side,
    listening, caring, inviting.
Thank you, Lord, for always being available to us
  whenever we need you.
Dear Lord, we're so glad that we know you.

Amen ✶

Silence

Lord, how can we possibly ever hear you,
 when our world is filled with so much noise?
 Our televisions, telephones, stereos, and radios
  seem to consume our attention.
 These noisy distractions not only make it difficult
  for us to pray and speak to you—
   they make it almost impossible for us
    to hear your word and guidance.
 They also tend to drown out all the beautiful sounds
  you have placed in this world of ours:
   the song of the birds,
   the wind in the trees,
   the sound of the waves on the shore.
Lord, let us learn to appreciate
 not only the sounds of your world
  but also the sound of silence.
 Let us learn to occasionally take a breather
  to sit in the silence and beauty of your world
   and make ourselves open
    to your voice alone.
We believe, Lord, that there are ways
 you are able to speak to us and guide us.
 We believe that those wonderful thoughts
  that make us feel so enlightened and good—
   come from you.
So speak to us, Lord,
 as we take a little time each day
  to sit quietly,
  to connect our thoughts with yours.

Amen ✠

IV

Facing Life

Happiness

Sometimes, Lord, we think that we'll finally be happy,
　　if only we get some particular thing that we want
　　or if things would happen the way we want them to.
　　We keep waiting for all the "if onlys" in our lives,
　　　　and when they don't occur,
　　　　　　we become disappointed and unhappy.
　　Why is it so hard for us to realize
　　　　that happiness isn't brought about
　　　　　　by the things that happen to us
　　　　　　　　but rather by the way we react
　　　　　　　　　　to the things that come our way?
Remind us, Lord, that we are the ones
　　who choose how we will react.
　　We can react to things with a good attitude
　　　　or a bad attitude,
　　　　　　with acceptance and satisfaction,
　　　　　　　　or resentment and bitterness.
　　We can open our minds and see the bright side of life
　　　　or narrow our vision and see only the darkness.
Teach us, Lord, to meet the events in our lives
　　with an openness and eagerness that will enable us
　　　　to feel hopeful rather than despairing,
　　　　challenged rather than discouraged,
　　　　and content rather than discontent.
Let us learn, Lord, how to find a bit of happiness
　　in each and every day of our lives.

Amen ✠

Humor

Lord, you have blessed us with the gift of laughter.
Let each of us learn to use this precious gift
to lighten our load and brighten our days.
Help us, Lord, to develop a really good sense of humor.
There are times when we tend to take
certain events a bit too seriously,
to regard them with a negative point of view.
We often get so concerned about the silly mistakes
we make
and the embarrassing moments we experience
that we completely miss the humor in them.
We forget that something embarrassing today
can provide us with a good laugh tomorrow.
Let us learn how to lighten up a bit, Lord,
to laugh and not be afraid,
to poke a little fun at ourselves.
Teach us, dear Lord,
to see the lighter, brighter side of things,
to enjoy life to its fullest.
Let us share our laughter with others,
to bring a bit of fun and pleasure
into the lives of those we know.
Let us always make sure, however,
that our humor is never offensive or hurtful
to anyone.
Remind us to be careful
to laugh with—and not at—others.
We thank you, Lord,
for all the times life gives us a chuckle.

Amen ✠

The Good and the Bad

When things go wrong, Lord, we often allow ourselves
 to become terribly depressed and discouraged.
 We want our lives to be constantly sunny and good,
  but life just isn't like that, is it, Lord?
 It's a mixture of good and bad,
  of highs and lows,
   of pleasures and pains.
Let us learn, Lord, to accept the fact that life—
 everybody's life—
   is not only difficult and sad at times,
    it's often unfair.
 Let us realize that we can't just accept the good parts
  and refuse to face the bad.
 To enjoy a full life, we must embrace all of it—
  its annoyances and problems,
   as well as its pleasures and joys;
  its disappointments and failures,
   as well as its successes and triumphs.
Teach each of us, Lord, how to appreciate the good
 and to learn and grow from facing and
  coping with the bad.
Lord, give us the strength and confidence we need
 to accept and embrace all of life.

Amen ✠

Change

Lord, from year to year our lives keep changing.
Each year brings new and different experiences,
new classes, new jobs, new friends, new activities.
We're constantly confronted with new phases
in our lives,
and we usually look forward to them eagerly.
But there are times, Lord,
when we become so comfortable with the old
that we find it difficult to adjust to the new.
Sometimes we're afraid of all the changes
that life brings our way.
We ask you, Lord, to take away our fears
and give us the confidence we need
to step out eagerly and try new things.
Give us the courage
to be ready and willing to take a few risks.
Let us realize that a safe, unchanging life—
a life without risks—
can be dull.
Don't let us be afraid
to risk failure in pursuit of success,
to risk disappointment in search of contentment,
to risk sadness in our quest for happiness.
Fill each of us with a spirit of adventure
that will allow us to view challenges
as opportunities rather than obstacles.
Let us learn, dear God,
to look forward, confidently,
to each new phase in our lives.

Amen ✠

Simplicity

Lord, let us be grateful for all the simple things in life,
    for your wondrous sunrises and sunsets,
    for your trees, your moon, your stars and planets.
    Let us be grateful for your woodlands, deserts,
        waterways, and meadows.
    Let us be grateful for the song of the bird,
        the touch of rain,
        the field of wildflowers,
        the billowy clouds.
    Let us be grateful for the warmth of friends,
        the comfort of a good book,
        the desire to learn.
Lord, bless those of us who cannot or will not fully enjoy
    these simple things that we so easily take for granted.
        Bless those of us
            who cannot speak, see, hear, walk, or learn.
        Bless those of us who are weak, ill, or confined.
        Bless those of us who are old and helpless.
We thank you, Lord, for all the simple things
    that are part of your creation,
        that you have so generously given us.

Amen ✠

Priorities

Lord, give us the wisdom we need
    to keep our priorities straight,
    to know what's truly important in life.
    At times, we begin to believe that
        only when we possess all the nice things we want,
            will we become satisfied—happy.
    Let us realize that material possessions
        will not bring us happiness.
Dear God, don't let us ever get caught up
    in a frantic and futile race to acquire "things."
    Make us wise;
        let us recognize our most precious possessions.
    Let us realize that our sense of worth is important,
        that our ability to do our jobs well
            and our ability to meet and face our challenges
              will bring us a sense of fulfillment.
    Let us realize that our relationships are important,
        that our ability to share love with family and friends,
            our ability to make others smile,
            will make our lives richer.
Let us realize, Lord, that a close relationship with you
    is the most important part of life,
        that knowing you
            and feeling ourselves precious in your sight,
            will make our lives secure,
              will give us a sense of confidence.
We thank you, Lord, for giving us the opportunity
    to know and enjoy
        all these precious and important things in our lives.

Amen ✠

V

Our
Relationship
With One
Another

Acceptance

Lord, teach us to accept each member of our family,
    to accept them all
        just as they are.
    There are times when we get annoyed and impatient
        with one another's faults and weaknesses.
        We often expect others to be perfect
           when we are far from perfect ourselves.
Teach us, Lord,
    to overlook one another's faults,
        to be more understanding and considerate
           of one another's weaknesses,
              to be more tolerant
                of one another's mistakes.
    Let us learn how to pay more attention
        to the good in one another
        rather than to the bad.
    There are times when we tend to forget that
        our family puts up with
           our own faults and imperfections—
              day after day.
    Remind us to be just,
        to tolerate the imperfections in others
           as they must tolerate imperfections in us.
If we ever begin to feel, Lord, that our family
    is hard to live with and hard to love,
        remind us that there are times
           when we, too, are hard to live with,
           when we, too, are hard to love.

Amen ✠

Sensitivity

Let us learn, Lord, how to be more sensitive
 to one another's feelings.
 Yes, there are times when we can't understand
  why others feel as they do.
Help us, Lord,
 to be more understanding of one another,
  to go out of our way to be patient and tolerant
   of the things we find difficult
    to understand.
Teach us, Lord, to be especially careful
 to never say or do things
  that will make others feel
   hurt, degraded, or discouraged.
Teach us also, Lord, to be more aware
 of one another's feelings,
  to notice when others are troubled,
   frightened, frustrated, or lonely.
 Give us eyes and hearts to see and feel
  the fatigue and frustrations of others,
   to be willing to offer a helping hand
    and caring heart.
 Let us notice when others struggle
  so that we can make ourselves available to listen,
   to offer encouragement.
 Let us realize when others need
  a pat on the back or a comforting hug
   so that we can reach out to them.

Amen ✠

Frustrations

Lord, there are days
   when we feel terribly crabby and frustrated.
   There are times when we feel angry and upset
      with someone or something—
         or everyone and everything.
         What do we do?
We usually take it out on those who are near us,
   mostly on the other members of our family.
   It seems that whenever we feel bad,
      we want those around us to feel bad too.
   Why do we so often take our frustrations out
      on one another?
   Why do we treat the people who are the closest to us
      so rudely, with so little consideration?
It isn't fair of us, is it, Lord?
   We wouldn't dare treat our friends in this manner,
      yet we expect our family to put up with it,
         to remain loyal and loving.
Teach us, Lord,
   to treat our family fairly.
   Teach us to work out our frustrations
      in less hurtful ways.
   Let us learn to be nicer to our family,
      especially when we don't feel like being nice.

Amen ✠

Talking and Listening

Teach us, Lord, to talk to one another openly, pleasantly.
    Let us learn how
        to listen to one another patiently.
    We confess to being impatient and intolerant
        of other's views.
    We tend to think that alternate viewpoints
        are either wrong, stupid, or less valid.
When we are narrow-minded and arrogant, Lord,
    and belittle and make fun of one another's opinions,
        teach us to listen to one another's views,
            to take a genuine interest in them.
                Perhaps we'll gain some understanding.
Let us also learn, Lord, to be open and trusting,
    to share our own concerns, interests, and dreams.
        Let us trust that others are interested in our lives.
Let us remember, however, to respect one another's privacy
    by keeping to ourselves
        the things that are told to us in confidence.
We ask you, Lord, to give us patience to be available,
    to listen to one another's concerns, doubts, and fears.
Bless us with your wisdom
    to communicate understanding and encouragement,
        support and love.

Amen ✠

Being Pleasant

Lord, at times it's hard to live so closely
    with others in a way that isn't annoying.
    Let us realize, however, that there's a big difference
        between being accidentally annoying
            and being deliberately mean and nasty.
    There are times when, instead of trying to get along,
        we feel spiteful and mean,
            quick and eager to start an argument.
    At times, Lord, we even go out of our way
        to tease, torment, and make fun of one another.
Let us realize our childishness.
    Let us see how petty we are when we're mean.
    Teach us to
        be kinder, nicer,
            more pleasant to one another.
Whenever we're tempted to be mean and outspoken, Lord,
    remind us of the love our family shares.
    Touch our hearts with an awareness
        of the bond we share as family—
            even when—
                especially when—
                    we're not especially pleasant.

Amen ✠

Disagreements

Since we are all unique individuals, Lord,
 who face life in different ways,
  we will disagree.
Let us learn, Lord, to disagree
 without hurting and offending one another.
 When we argue, we often let our anger take over;
  we tend to say mean and hurtful things.
 At times, our arguments end up being nothing more
  than rude and angry shouting matches—
   no one listening, no one caring.
Lord, we are going to argue;
 teach us to argue maturely and fairly.
 Teach us to be honest,
  to admit when we're wrong,
  to cease arguing unreasonably.
 Teach us to hold our tongue,
  to give others a chance to express their views,
  to listen with an open mind.
We ask you, Lord, to give us the ability
 to avoid blaming others for "starting a fight."
 May we be fair in accepting blame and
  offering apologies.
Teach us, Lord, to be less concerned about
  winning arguments
 and more concerned about learning something
  from them.
 May we use our disagreements
  to better understand one another.

Amen ✤

Apologies and Forgiveness

Lord, the little skirmishes we have
 often turn into long, drawn-out battles
  filled with anger, bitterness, and resentment.
 Let us be quick to apologize,
  quick to forgive.
 It's often hard to say "I'm sorry,"
  and we so often delay,
   allowing unnecessary resentments to build.
Teach us, Lord, to be willing to apologize,
 even when we're not completely at fault.
 Let us learn to be big enough and kind enough
  to apologize quickly and sincerely—
   especially when we've hurt someone.
 Let us also learn to be gracious enough
  to accept the apologies offered us:
   "As we forgive those who trespass against us."
 There are times when we feel hurt and offended
  and don't really want to be forgiving.
 At times, we want to hang on to our anger,
  nurse our resentments,
  and feel totally self-pitying,
   perhaps even vengeful.
Especially, then, Lord, let us realize
 how destructive and damaging these feelings can be
  to those we love, to our family, to ourselves.
   For these emotions have the power
    to eat away at us.
Give us the ability, Lord,
 to be as forgiving to others as you are to us.

Amen ✠

VI
Daily Responsibilities

Cooperation

Lord, let us remember to always try to do our best
   to make our day to-day living experiences
      easier for one another.
Remind us, Lord, to be considerate
   of one another's privacy and space,
      to have regard for one another's belongings.
Let us realize how pleasant family life will be
    if only we are willing to share
      and keep things in order.
Lord, help us remember
   to avoid leaving our personal belongings lying around:
      our toys, radios, books, clothes.
         They clutter space; they cause others to trip.
Remind us to clean up after ourselves in the kitchen
    and the bathroom
    so that others might enjoy a tidy place.
Remind us to put tools and other household belongings
    back where others can easily find them.
        How annoying it is to search for misplaced keys,
          to move bicycles out of the way,
            to pick up scattered newspapers.
Remind us to be courteous when we use the phone,
    the bathroom, the television.
Remind us to be thoughtful of those who care for us,
    who wait to hear from us,
    who watch for us when we're late.
Remind us, Lord,
    to be fair about doing everything we can
      to make life easier for one another.

Amen ✠

Chores

Lord, most of our chores aren't fun to do.
    In fact, many of them are a real pain and inconvenience.
        What's more, there are so many,
            so much that has to be done all the time,
            and so little time.
    Parents work hard to keep home and family
        running smoothly.
        Children have their school responsibilities,
            part-time jobs, and other activities.
    Let us realize that it is a matter of justice
        that we all do our fair share—
            and more when needed.
Remind us, Lord, that we can't expect others
        to be our servants,
    that we can't just take—and never give.
    Let each of us learn
        to accept our fair share of family chores—
            especially those chores that are the least likable,
            the most tedious.
Let us learn, Lord,
    to pull our fair share of the load in our family
    without complaining, without procrastinating.
    Don't let us be tempted to wait around
        for others to do the things we ought to do.
We ask you, Lord, to give each of us the ability
    to do our chores with a feeling of accomplishment
        rather than with an attitude of resentment.
    Teach us how to cooperate as a family
        to keep our home and family running smoothly.

Amen ✠

Finances

Lord, we sometimes lose sight of what we can afford.
  We want things that others have:
    a new car, outfit, bicycle, or baseball mitt.
      When we hear "we can't afford it,"
        how quick we are to get upset and sulk.
Let us realize, Lord, how hard it is to finance a family.
  Let us show our appreciation to those who labor,
    with devotion and selflessness,
      to provide financial resources for our family.
        Let us not be demanding.
When we let our selfish wants
  make unfair demands on our family's finances,
    show us your way, Lord.
May we never make others feel guilty
  because our selfish wants can't be met.
Let us realize that we don't necessarily need things
  simply because our friends or neighbors have them.
Let us learn to be satisfied to live within our means,
  to be willing to make sacrifices—
    without complaining—
      when our family's finances are tight
      or troubled.
Help each of us, Lord, to develop a sense of thrift
    and a healthy respect for the value of money.
  Let us learn to budget our money wisely
    so that the basic needs of our family will always
      be met,
    so that we have the resources to offer
      financial support to those in need.

Amen ✠

Rules

There are times, Lord,
    when we feel that our family rules and regulations
        are much too strict—
            even unfair.
    At times, we feel that more is expected of us
        than other families expect of their members.
    We know that certain rules and restrictions
        are necessary to keep order in the life of a family,
            but there are times when we just don't like
                being told what we can and can't do.
Teach us, Lord,
    to respect rules that are fair and reasonable—
        even if we don't especially like them.
    Let us realize that rules exist
        to make life easier, safer, better.
            Rules exist to protect us from harm and trouble,
                to shield us from emotional or physical injury.
    When we begin to envy others
        because their family enjoys more "freedom,"
            let us remember that too much "freedom"
                leads to problems—
                    even tragedies.
Teach us, Lord, to live with our family's rules,
    even if we don't totally agree with them.
    Let us learn to be thankful
        that we have people in our lives
            who care enough about us
                to make these rules for us—
                    and insist that we respect them.

Amen ✠

VII

Learning
How
to Live

Failure

Lord, we understand why we fail
    when we don't try our best.
        But we find it hard to accept our failures
            when we give our all and still fail.
    You'd think that success would naturally follow
        a sincere attempt to do well—
            but it doesn't always.
Teach us, Lord, to handle our failures
    without getting totally discouraged.
    May we realize that everyone struggles with failure,
        and most people manage to survive,
            holding on to hope.
When we fail, Lord,
    be our encouragement to continue.
        Give us the strength to pick ourselves up
            and try again—and again.
        Bring to mind those countless others
            who have kept on trying,
            who kept on hoping.
Let us learn to regard our failures, Lord,
    not as setbacks,
        but as opportunities for learning new ways
            to face our challenges.
Stay beside us, Lord,
    and help us meet life's challenges
        with a strong, positive, and determined attitude.

Amen ✠

Helpfulness

We always enjoy and appreciate other people's help;
  but when our chance to be helpful comes along,
    we're often too lazy, too selfish, or too busy.
      It's so much easier to sit back
        and let someone else
          help with the dishes,
            carry out the garbage,
              or run the errands.
Oh, Lord, let us learn to be generous with ourselves,
  to offer help when we can.
  Let us learn to be kind and unselfish,
    to do favors without expecting something in return.
Teach us, Lord, to take care of one another,
  to help when others are too tired or overworked,
  to help with homework when someone is confused,
  to help with repairs when something is broken,
  to care for those who are too ill—
    or too young—
      to care for themselves.
Build our awareness of the needs around us
      every day
      and inspire us to help without being asked.
Let us learn, Lord, to take care of one another
  with generosity, love, kindness, and self-giving.

Amen ✠

A Positive Attitude

Lord, we know that there are things in life
    that simply can't be changed;
        no amount of wishing will change the circumstances;
        no amount of hoping can erase the past.
    But some things can be changed: our attitudes.
Let us realize, Lord, that the attitudes
    with which we face life's unchangeable events
        can always be changed.
    Remind us that these attitudes
        are a matter of choice—
            our choice.
    We can choose to meet problems with worry and
            despair—
        or with hope and confidence.
    We can choose to meet challenges with fear and
            trembling—
        or with eagerness and anticipation.
    We can choose to meet disappointment with protest
            and spite—
        or with courage and a sense of humor.
    We can choose to meet life with suspicion and
            resentment—
        or with hope and a positive outlook.
    We can choose to be content—
        or discontent and bitter.
Let us realize, Lord, that if we choose
    to develop the right attitudes,
        life will always be promising.

Amen ✠

Openness

Lord, there are times when we desperately want our lives
    to move in a certain direction.
    We find it hard to cope with things
        that don't turn out exactly as we prefer.
    Why is it so hard to accept life as it is?
Teach us, Lord, to go with the flow,
    to roll with the punches,
    to have trust and faith in you.
    Instead of begging you to make things happen
        to our liking,
            let us learn to be open
                to the opportunities and challenges
                    that you wish to send us.
    Instead of pleading with you to change life for us,
        let us learn to ask for the strength and wisdom
            we need
            to face whatever comes.
We feel confident, Lord,
    that if we rely on your help and guidance,
        you will show us how to cope with any challenge
            that life puts before us.
    We believe that trust in your care
        will help us handle
            whatever life has in store for us.

Amen ✠

Criticism

Lord, help us to handle constructive criticism.
    We often feel resentful when others
        point out our errors
            or tell us how something should be done.
    Help us to realize that when people give advice,
        they intend to be helpful
            rather then critical.
    Help us to realize that we can often learn a great deal
        from the experience of others.
Give us the ability, Lord,
    to be open to the advice of others,
    to view their advice as gift
        rather than annoyance.
    May we even become grateful for the opportunity
        to learn new ways
            of facing and coping with life.
We also ask you, Lord,
    to teach us how to give constructive criticism
        without offending or hurting.
    Although we don't usually like to receive criticism,
        seldom do we hesitate to offer it.
    We know we tend to criticize too harshly,
        to say things that are mean, degrading, and hurtful.
        Give us the ability to see how wrong it is
            to put someone down,
            to make fun of someone.
Dear Lord, remind us to give constructive criticism
    with kindness and a sincere desire to be helpful—
        rather than hurtful.

Amen ✠

Compromise

Keep reminding us, Lord, that we can't always have
    our way.
    We are a family,
        and each of us has different interests,
            different points of view,
            different insights,
            different preferences,
            different ways of coping with life.
    Let us remember to respect one another's individuality,
        for each of us is unique, equally important,
            and totally deserving of respect.
    Let us realize that although other people's ways
        may not be the best for us,
            they are often as "right" and as "good" as ours.
Teach us, Lord, to accommodate one another
        when our views and interests conflict.
    May we grow to respect our differences,
        with minds that are open and unprejudiced,
        with a willingness to compromise.
Teach us, Lord, the loving art of compromising.
    Let us meet one another halfway in every issue;
        let us be willing to consider and respect
            the wishes and desires of others—
                even if those wishes do not agree with ours.
Let us learn, Lord, to be kind and unselfish
    in ways that foster justice and cooperation.

Amen ✠

Convictions

Lord, we often hesitate to speak out
　　for the things we believe in—
　　　　especially if our beliefs don't happen to be popular.
After all, we don't want others to think
　　that we're old-fashioned,
　　that we're not broad-minded.
Let us realize, Lord, that being unwisely
　　and recklessly broad-minded, however, is never a virtue.
　　　　Give us the wisdom to choose our beliefs carefully
　　　　　　and the confidence to speak out
　　　　　　　　in support of those beliefs.
　　　　Give us the courage to speak out
　　　　　　for morality,
　　　　　　for respect,
　　　　　　for life,
　　　　　　for family values.
　　　　Give us the courage to speak out
　　　　　　against ignorance,
　　　　　　against prejudice,
　　　　　　against injustice.
When we are intimidated by what others think of us,
　　give us the words to state our beliefs
　　　　with confidence, courage, and wisdom.

Amen ✠

VIII

Living With Our Feelings

Moodiness

Lord, there are times when our moods
    go up and down like an elevator.
    One minute we're sitting on top of the world—
        all happy and satisfied—
            and then something unpleasant happens—
            often something small and unimportant—
                and we slide into a gloomy mood.
Our emotions go up and down
    and round and round
        in dizzying circles.
            It's so confusing!
We ask you, Lord, to teach us to handle our moods.
    Help us to realize that life isn't constant,
        that life has its cycles,
        its "up" periods, its "down" periods.
Teach each of us, Lord, to live through the "down" periods
    without getting too discouraged,
    without losing our ability to look forward
        eagerly and confidently
            to the "up" periods
                that do eventually come.
Lord, bless us with the grace
    to accept and live
        with both the sunny and rainy periods in our lives.
    Let us remember that
        both sunshine and showers make the rainbow.

Amen ✠

Fear

There are so many things in life that are scary, Lord.
    We see the troubles that other people have,
        and we find it hard to believe
            that we could ever be strong with the
              same problems.
    In fact, we often doubt
        that we'll ever be confident enough
           to meet all the demands
              that life brings our way.
    How often we hesitate to face certain events
        because we're afraid we'll get hurt,
           afraid we'll fail,
           afraid we'll make fools of ourselves.
When we become timid and draw back, Lord,
    remind us of all the experiences,
        all the triumphs,
        all the excitement,
        all the life,
           we might miss
              by trying to avoid hurt or failure.
Lord, grant us a trust that is our companion
    when those difficult times come.
    May we believe in you, in your presence to us;
        may we cling to a confidence in your love for us.
    Let us believe, wholeheartedly,
        that you are beside us
           in all the problems and uncertainties of life.

Amen ✠

Self-Pity

Lord, we realize that disappointments
  are a normal part of life.
  But when something disappointing happens to us,
   we don't know how to handle it.
  When things go wrong,
   we so often get discouraged;
   we want to sit back and feel sorry for ourselves.
Let us realize, Lord, how useless is the pastime of self-pity.
  It's a negative, crippling, self-defeating emotion.
   We know that life isn't easy,
    that it certainly isn't always fair.
   Armed with that knowledge,
    may we learn to accept difficulties and unfairness
    without getting depressed.
Remind us, Lord, that sadness is part of the fabric of life,
  as is the joy of accomplishment,
  the excitement of challenges and new adventures,
  the pleasures of companionship and friendship,
  the warmth and comfort of love.
Teach us, Lord, to focus on these good things
  and to take life's disappointments and frustrations
   as part of the total experience of being alive.
  Make us smart enough and strong enough
   to learn from our disappointments,
   to put them behind us,
   and to move quickly and confidently
    on to better things.

Amen ✠

Anger

Lord, teach us to deal with anger and resentment.
When someone hurts us or offends us,
it so easy to be angry and resentful—
rather than patient and forgiving.
Sometimes we feel that we actually have a right
to feel bitter, resentful, and unforgiving.
Sometimes we take pleasure
in feeling angry and vengeful,
even though it's ultimately self-destructive.
Let us realize, Lord, that our anger often hurts us
more than it hurts others.
Anger has the power
to keep us from enjoying life;
it tears us apart,
leaving us isolated and alone—
separated from you, Lord.
Teach us, Lord, to set ourselves free
when we're tempted to imprison ourselves
in our self-centered, self-righteous
cells of anger and hatred.
Help us to be as generous with our forgiveness
as you are with yours.
Let us remember that forgiveness
has the power to make our lives sweeter,
more peaceful,
more centered on you,
more enjoyable.

Amen ✠

Contentment

Lord, we're quick to bring
  our problems, troubles, and sorrows to you.
  But when life is good and we're having fun,
    we often forget about you.
We're really sorry for being so fickle, Lord.
  We want you to know that we are grateful,
    that we treasure our happy times as a family.
  We know you are a part of those times—
    yesterday, today, and tomorrow.
Be with us always, Lord,
  when we're together, playing games, watching television,
    entertaining friends.
  We invite you into our midst in all that we do:
    our picnics,
    our bike rides,
    our games,
    our parties,
    our family gatherings.
We thank you, Lord,
  for all the opportunities you give us
    to share and enjoy life
      with our family and
      with you.

Amen ✠

IX

Coping
With
Our
Faults

Jealousy

Lord, teach us how to deal with jealousy.
    Every once in a while,
        that green-eyed monster storms into our lives,
           and we become jealous of all the nice things
             other people have,
          all the exciting things
             other people get to do.
    We see only the pleasant things that happen to others
        and fail to notice their struggles.
    There are times when we fail to realize that
        we have as much good and bad in our lives—
           no more, no less—
             as those we envy.
Teach each of us, Lord, to control our jealousy,
    to be satisfied with our own plentiful blessings.
    Let us see that having more
        does not necessarily assure happiness.
Let us also realize, Lord,
    that jealousy doesn't just make us feel bad,
        it diminishes our integrity;
        it makes us small and petty in our humanness.
May we be content with our own lives,
    and may we be sincerely pleased and happy
        when something nice happens
           to our brothers and sisters and friends.

Amen ✠

Selfishness

Lord, help us control our natural tendencies to be selfish.
  We confess that there are times
      when we just don't feel like sharing,
      when we're much more concerned
          with our own satisfaction
              than with the needs and comforts
                  of others.
Let us learn how to be more generous, Lord,
    to share with others
        the things that we are fortunate enough to have.
    Let us learn to be kinder, more thoughtful,
        always ready to treat others
            as we ourselves would like to be treated.
    We often forget
        that sharing and giving pleasure to others
            has a tremendous power
                to bring us joy.
Lord, let us always remember
    that the happiest and most satisfied people in this world
        are those who are willing to give of themselves,
            of their time,
            their attention,
            their support,
            their love.
Teach us, Lord, your own unselfish ways.

Amen ✠

Honesty

Lord, it's so easy to see the faults in others,
    while overlooking our own.
    We're often quick to criticize others—
        but, oh, so slow to recognize
            when our own behavior is just as bad.
Let us learn, Lord, to stop fooling ourselves
    into believing that our faults aren't as bad
        or as annoying
            as the faults of others.
    Teach us how to take a good honest look at ourselves,
        to see ourselves as we really are.
    Bless us with inner sight
        that allows us to see ourselves as others see us.
    May we cease making excuses for our shortcomings.
    May we learn to change the things
        that should be changed
            so as to become the kind of people
                we can and should become.
Help each of us to grow up, Lord,
    to take full responsibility for our faults.
        Make us wise in the ways of our faults,
            honest enough to admit them,
                courageous enough to face them,
                    and strong enough to change them.

Amen ✠

Pride

Lord, there is nothing wrong in being proud
        of a job well done.
    Sometimes, however, we tend to get vain
        about what we know we can do.
    Sometimes, we get proud and arrogant
        about who and what we are.
    Sometimes we begin to think
        that we're better than others.
When we fall into this bad habit, Lord,
    fill us with an awareness of your love for each of us,
        an equal love in which we all share.
    May we never loose sight of the fact
        that any talents we possess
            are purely gifts you've given us,
            gifts that bring with them
                not a right to be prideful
                but an obligation
                    to develop the gift
                        for the good of others.
We are grateful, Lord,
    for all the precious gifts and talents
        you have granted us.
    May we use them wisely and productively
        rather than proudly and boastfully.

Amen ✠

Worry

Lord, how unwise it is to worry,
  to waste our time and energy so uselessly.
How often do we look back
  and worry about the past—
    and look ahead
      to worry about the future?
Let us realize, Lord, that the past is finished—
  and usually quickly forgotten by most people—
    and the future is simply too uncertain
      to waste our time worrying about.
When we begin to worry about future misfortunes,
  remind us about those times
    when we exhausted our energy
      worrying about something that,
        in the end,
          never occurred.
Teach us, Lord, that the only thing
  we can possibly do anything about
    is the present.
Call us into the present—
  to live one day at a time,
    fully and well.
Bless us, Lord, with the faith and confidence we need
  to know that you are always available
    to help us face tomorrow—
      when tomorrow arrives.

Amen ✠

Complaints

Instead of being thankful for all the things we have, Lord,
    we so often complain about what we don't have.
    When things go wrong,
        we often give in
            to a sense of dissatisfaction
                that gradually takes over our lives.
    We allow the dissatisfaction to blind us
        to the wondrous good that surrounds us.
Let us realize, Lord, that no one likes to listen
    to our sulking and whining complaints.
        Not only is it annoying
          but it's unfair for us
            to force others
                to endure our complaints.
    We have no right to drag others down
        with a negative, complaining view of life.
When we begin to complain, Lord,
    remind us to think about those
        who have problems much worse than ours.
    Teach us to meet each day with a more positive outlook,
        an outlook that will make our days much more
          enjoyable.
May we always remember, Lord, that we control
    our own sense of contentment and discontentment.
        We have the power
          to make ourselves more willing to be satisfied.
Lord, the next time we are tempted to complain,
    stop us with your grace;
        remind us to count our blessings instead.

Amen ✠

X

Living
With
Others

Love

Lord, it's so easy to love those who are nice to us,
    who always agree with us,
    who do things the way we think they ought to be done.
But, Lord, there are some people
    who are extremely hard to understand,
    who are annoying and irritating,
    who are really hard for us to love.
When we tend to be unkind
        and unloving to such people,
      remind us of those times when we, too, are
        annoying,
        exasperating,
        hard to understand,
        difficult to love.
Teach us, Lord, to focus on the good in others.
    Teach us to see their needs
      rather than their weaknesses.
    Let us realize that all of us are annoying and irritating
      when our burdens begin to overwhelm us.
    May we learn to love with patience and compassion
      allowing others to be imperfect—
        especially given the fact
          that we are most imperfect ourselves.
You love us just as we are, Lord;
    let us love in the same fashion,
      for those who are the least lovable among us
        often need our love the most.

Amen ✠

Prejudice

Lord, you have created a world that is a dwelling place
    for all kinds of people—
        people of many races,
        many religions,
        many cultures.
    How sad that the appearance and ways of others
        are difficult for us to accept and understand.
We confess, Lord, that we are suspicious of the differences.
    We beg you to guard us from ignorance and arrogance;
        may we never feel "better" than others.
    Protect us from being prejudiced,
        from turning a blind eye
            to the prejudice that others display.
    Never allow us to hesitate to speak up
        when we see others being treated unfairly, unjustly.
Give us, Lord, the strength we need
    to stand up for the equality and beauty of all peoples.
As the Creator of all humankind,
    you expect us to accept and love all your people.
        May we always do just that.

Amen ✠

Gossip

Lord, help us to be considerate of others,
    to avoid talking and gossiping about them.
    Let us learn to treat our friends and neighbors
        as we would like them to treat us.
    There are times when we give in to a mean streak,
        when we speak badly about the people we know.
    Deep down, we realize how cruel and destructive
        this can be,
            but so often, for some reason,
            we do it anyway.
Why do we act like this, Lord?
    Is it because we enjoy informing people about
        the faults and mistakes and weaknesses of others?
    Is it because we feel that in tearing others down,
        we raise ourselves up?
    Let us realize how mistaken this type of thinking is,
        how unfair it is to criticize others
        when we don't do everything right ourselves.
    Let us be aware of how hurtful and harmful gossip is
        to the people about whom we talk
        and also to ourselves.
    For the grime of gossip
        settles on those who gossip as well.
We ask you, Lord, to teach us kindness and consideration.

Amen ✠

Blessings

Lord, we are so blessed.
 We know the comforts of our family,
  the peace of our home.
 Yet, countless people live in loneliness and fear,
  with hunger and disease,
   surrounded by the threats of war and death.
 Here we are with opportunities for life, education,
  freedom, peace, health…
   why?
Why are we so blessed, Lord?
 Why are we here
  instead of in a place that is plagued
   with hunger
   or the lack of freedom
   or the horrors of war?
  Do we deserve to be here, to enjoy this abundance?
  Is it just an accident of birth?
Or perhaps, Lord, it is a gift of birth,
 a gift from you.
 It makes us wonder if all the privileges
  we've been granted
 come hand in hand with tremendous
   responsibilities—
  the responsibility to feed others,
  the responsibility to educate others,
  the responsibility to bring peace.
Dear Lord, we promise to do everything we can
 to use our blessings and opportunities
  to do good in this world.

Amen ✠

Neighborliness

Lord, teach each of us to be good neighbors.
    Yes, there are people living in our community
        who are not especially friendly,
        who are often hard to understand.
    There are people, indeed,
        whom we don't like.
    Teach us to overlook the faults and frailties
        of these people,
            to treat them in a neighborly way.
Because it isn't easy to be neighborly, Lord,
    we look to you to touch our hearts.
    Keep us from pulling blinders over our eyes,
        from "minding our own business."
            Let us see the needs of others.
Dear Lord, let us be mature enough
    to extend friendship to all our neighbors,
        next door, down the street, and around the world.
    May we take the time to
        visit with those who are lonesome,
        run errands for those who are old and feeble,
        brighten the day for someone who is ill,
        reach out to someone who is troubled,
        do a favor for an exhausted parent,
        play with a lonely child.
Teach each of us, Lord, to be a neighbor
    who is friendly, caring, helpful, and loving.

Amen ✠

Friendliness

Lord, we thank you for our friends.
  We consider ourselves blessed to have good friends;
    may we always be worthy of their friendship.
Lord, let us always give our love and respect
  to all these precious people in our lives.
  Teach us to treat our friends
    as lovingly as you treat us.
  Let us always remember to be loyal to them,
    to avoid hurting them or offending them,
      to avoid talking about them or making fun of them.
  Let us always remember
    to treat them fairly and compassionately,
    to avoid criticizing them for their faults,
    to refrain from being envious of their gifts,
    to be forgiving of their mistakes.
  Let us always be available
    to give our friends our time and attention,
    to lend our help and support,
      to share with them our pleasures and joys.
Dear Lord, teach us to love our friends with a love
  that is kind, generous, unselfish, and understanding.

Amen ✠

XI

Today's Problems and Standards

Values

Lord, we're surrounded by many disturbing influences.
  There's so much violence on television,
      so many stories and movies about people
          who have a warped and depraved sense of values.
  There are books, magazines—even lyrics in our music—
      that promote a distorted sense of morality.
  We even see our friends accepting values
      that are different from those our family believes.
  At times, it's really hard to know what's right.
Teach us, Lord, to know what to believe.
  Help us avoid being influenced
      by all the warped values that surround us.
  Let us always discuss questionable beliefs,
      to be open to the guidance of those
          who have had more experience in living
              than we have.
Teach us, Lord, to stand by and uphold our family's values,
  even if those values are not exactly popular.
  Make us realize that we don't have to be like sheep,
      blindly following the pack,
          especially when the values that others promote
              are not rooted in the gospel.
  Don't let us be afraid to be different
      if we must be different to be right.
Dear Lord, give us not only the wisdom we need
  to know what is right
      but also the strength we need
          to accept to do what is right.

Amen ✠

Alcohol

Lord, we know of people who actually depend on alcohol
   to help them have a good time.
   May we never be tempted to think that it's necessary
      to have a few drinks to have fun.
   Let us realize how destructive drinking can be,
      how badly it can affect our lives.
We know, Lord, that alcohol can impair our judgment
      and make us willing to do things we'd never do.
   We know that alcohol can make us take risks,
      can cause us to drive recklessly and irresponsibly.
   We know that alcohol can lead to tragic accidents.
   Don't let us fool ourselves into believing
      that we can handle alcohol
         without being affected by it.
   If we're ever tempted to think that alcohol has the power
      to make our lives easier and more exciting
         or that it has the power to soothe our pains
            and ease our disappointments,
               remind us, Lord, that its ability
                  to depress is a lot stronger
                     and longer lasting
                        than its ability
                           to soothe
                           or stimulate.
Help us, Lord, to avoid getting involved with people
   who think it's really okay to drink and get drunk.

Amen ✤

Drugs

Lord, help us to say "no" to drugs.
There are so many people who just won't believe
that drugs are dangerous.
They won't face the fact
that the short-lived "high" they get
usually ends in a depressing—
perhaps dangerous—
"low."
Nor will they admit
that their risk of getting addicted
is extremely high.
They kid themselves into thinking that
if they're careful, they won't get hooked.
Don't let us ever start thinking that way, Lord.
Open our minds to the facts:
there is no drug that is absolutely safe;
we can become dependent on even mild drugs;
all drugs can be harmful and damaging
to both our bodies and our minds.
Let us also always be aware of the trouble and the pain
that can be caused to both ourselves and our families,
not only because drugs are dangerous
but because they are also illegal.
Lead us away from situations
that would bring pain and shame to our family.
Lord, if anyone ever tempts us to go along with the crowd
and just give it a try,
let us be strong enough and smart enough
to say "no."

Amen ✤

Sex

Let us remember, Lord, that sex
    is a powerful and beautiful expression of love
        that should always be regarded with deep respect.
    Let us realize that sex provides us with the ability
        to show our deepest love for another person.
When we are tempted, Lord, to use sex
    in a way that may become a source of sorrow
        either for us or for someone we care for,
            be our guide.
Protect us, Lord, from being swayed
        by today's easy attitudes toward love and sex.
    Let us realize that it's not old-fashioned
        to regard sex as a sacred gift that should be reserved
            for the real love of marriage.
Remind us, Lord,
    that not only is sex outside of marriage unwise,
        it can be extremely unsafe—even deadly.
Let us also remember, Lord, that sex should never be used
    as a means of proving our love for someone.
        Anyone who wishes to use sex in this way
            is probably more interested
                in their own selfish gratification
                than in real love.
Let us always be smart enough, dear Lord,
    to choose the right beliefs and attitudes
        in regard to love and sex,
            keeping in mind that we and those we care for
                will have to live with whatever happens
                as a result of the choices we make.

Amen ✠

Peer Pressure

There are times, Lord, when instead of being true
    to our own sense of right and wrong,
        we tend to go along with the crowd.
At times, it's easier,
    so much more convenient,
        to go along with what everyone else
           is thinking and doing,
                in order to be accepted.
We often desperately wish to be part of the crowd.
Lord, give us the wisdom to know when it's bad
    to just blindly follow the leader.
Let each of us realize how dumb it is
    to go along with others,
        when we know in our hearts
           that what we're doing
             isn't right.
Let us realize that there are times
    when the price of popularity
        may be much more than we can afford,
           and a group that demands so high a price
           is not a group
              with which we should get involved.
Make each of us strong enough, Lord,
    to stand firmly behind our beliefs,
    to never value popularity
        over true friendship and ideals.

Amen ✠

Authority

Lord, there are some people who think it's cool
>   to disrupt a class,
>   to make trouble on the job,
>   to try to get away with whatever they can.
>   Some people have no respect for the rights of others,
>   for those who have the difficult job
>   of protecting the rights of all of us.
>   How chaotic our world would be if we had no laws,
>   no officials,
>   no one in authority
>   to keep order in our daily lives.
Remind us, Lord, that we each have an obligation
>   to help those in authority
>   keep order in our world
>   and to show them our respect.
>   May we not criticize
>   those who are trying to do a job
>   that we probably couldn't do
>   or wouldn't want to do.
>   Let us willingly accept the responsibility
>   of cooperating with and giving our support
>   to those who carry the burden of authority.
Lord, bless our teachers, bosses, pastors;
>   our law-enforcement officers and government officials;
>   and our parents.
>   Bless them all
>   and give them the strength
>   and wisdom they need
>   to do a good job for us.

Amen ✠

XII

Our
Goals
and
Achievements

Mission

Lord, we believe that we all come into this world
   with a unique purpose: a mission.
   We believe that each of us
      has something special to accomplish in our lifetime.
Guide us, Lord, and show us what you want us to do.
   There are so many people who do such great
      and important things in this world.
         We often wonder if what we do
            will be even remotely important.
   Help us to remember that
      even if we don't accomplish the kind of
         earth-changing things that others do,
            we have made our significant contribution—
               however small—
                  if we have made the lives of some
                  a bit easier,
                  a bit happier.
Let us be grateful for our talents and abilities.
Let us be open to your guidance and direction,
   always ready and willing to do what we can
      to make this world a little better than it is.
And if we ever happen to feel overwhelmed
   by visions of great feats we must achieve,
      remind us that it was never your intention
         to have us accomplish our life's work
            alone and unaided.
Dear Lord, give us the help and guidance we need
   to accomplish whatever you expect us to accomplish.

Amen ✠

Effort

Help us, Lord, to always put our best effort
  into our studies,
  our jobs,
  our chores,
  and any project or activity we undertake.
  Sometimes we get lazy and do just enough to get by,
    without really making an effort
      to do the best we can.
  Let us realize that we don't have to be geniuses
    or perfectionists to do a good job;
      we just have to be willing
        to give it our best effort.
Dear Lord, when we are tempted to be lazy,
  inject us with a good dose of energy and ambition.
  When we feel that things are too difficult for us,
    let us ask for the help or the advice that we need.
  When we feel that we're failing,
    don't let us be tempted to give up—
      or to give in to cheating.
  When we feel discouraged,
    let us remember your promise
      to help us with all of life's struggles.
  Give us, Lord, the wisdom, the desire,
    and the ambition we need
      to put forth our best effort
        in everything we undertake.
And remind us, Lord,
  that we will get out of our lives
    only as much as we are willing to put into them.

Amen ✠

Competition

Let us always be careful, Lord,
 to keep a sense of fairness in all our sports and games.
 We sometimes get so obsessed
  with competing and winning
   that we lose sight of playing
    with true respectful competition.
 At times, we even lose sight of having fun.
Yes, it feels great to win, Lord, but help us remember
 that we can also get a feeling of accomplishment
  from knowing that we played fairly
   and gave it our very best.
 Let us remember that we can enjoy and share
  in the triumph of achievement,
   even when we lose.
Let us also remember, Lord,
 never to allow any talents we possess
  to go to our heads,
  to make us vain and arrogant.
 Teach us to play for the good of the team
  rather than for our own personal pride.
 And don't let us ever be guilty of belittling
  those who are less talented than we are.
Let us learn, Lord, to play fairly so that—
 win or loose—
  everyone enjoys the sport.

Amen ✠

Challenge and Opportunity

Lord, life is full of challenge and opportunity.
There are times when it all seems so exciting
and we feel ambitious and confident,
ready and eager to meet any opportunity
that may come our way.
And then there are those other times
when we feel totally inadequate and incapable
of handling the challenges of life.
Give us the confidence we need, Lord,
to accept the challenges that come into our lives,
and give us the enthusiasm we need
to regard each new experience in life
as an exciting adventure.
Make us strong enough to reach out eagerly and
fearlessly
to each new experience that presents itself to us
so that we may never have any regrets
about missed opportunities.
Help us, Lord, to do all we can
to prepare ourselves both physically and mentally
to meet all the challenges that will come our way.
Help us Lord,
to keep our bodies healthy and strong,
our minds open and disciplined,
our attitudes positive and forward looking,
and our faith and trust in your help
solid and confident.

Amen ✠

Hopes and Dreams

When everything goes right and life runs smoothly, Lord,
    we tend to be satisfied and confident.
    But when things begin to go wrong and life gets tough,
        we get upset and discouraged.
Let each of us learn, Lord,
    how to face life's difficulties and disappointments
        with a more positive and hopeful view.
Teach us how to accept
    the disillusioning things in life,
        and not become disillusioned.
Teach us how to deal with hopes
    that remain unrealized,
        and not stop hoping.
Teach us how to cope with wishes
    that are not granted,
        and not stop wishing.
Teach us how to live with dreams
    that remain unfulfilled,
        and not stop dreaming.

Amen ✶

XIII

Prayers
for
Special
Needs

A Problem

Lord, we come to you with joined hands and hearts
    to ask for your help in solving the problem
        that our family is facing.
    Now, more than ever, we all need
        your loving help and support.
We have faith, Lord, that you will give each of us
    the wisdom to handle this.
    We believe that you will give us
        the strength and confidence we all need
            to meet this problem
                with courage,
                determination,
                and cooperation.
Protect each of us, Lord, from being tempted
        to give in to discouragement and defeat.
    Show us how to resolve this problem
        and to comfort and support one another
            as we try to work our way through
                this difficult time.
We believe, Lord, that with your help,
    we will have the ability to face
        whatever happens as a result of this problem.
Help us, dear Lord, to accept the solution
    that you think is best for us.

Amen ✠

An Illness

Lord, we ask you to bless (n)
    and to use your healing power
        not only to make (n) well again
            but to help him[her] get through this illness
            without undue discomfort and
            discouragement.
We also ask you to give (n)
    the strength and determination
        to do everything he[she] needs to do
            to regain health as soon as possible.
We often take our health for granted, Lord,
    and don't do what's best for our own well-being.
        Then when we're struck down and feeling sick,
        we tend to feel sorry for ourselves.
Teach us, Lord, to get through our illnesses
    with more patience and endurance,
    with an attitude that is positive and confident.
    Teach us to accept the responsibility
        of always doing everything we can
        to keep ourselves healthy.
And let us always remember, Lord,
    to be grateful for the life
        with which you have blessed us,
            whatever physical conditions that might include.
We pray that your healing power
    will comfort (n)
        and all of us.

Amen ✠

Sadness and Grief

Oh, Lord, we have experienced a great loss in our lives,
  and we don't know how to handle it.
  There's an ache in our hearts that won't go away.
    It's there every minute of every day.
    It's there when we wake up in the dark,
      lonely stillness of the night.
Help us, Lord, to cope with it.
  Let us learn how to work our way through
    this sadness and grief
      without getting bitter,
      without losing faith,
      without blaming you.
  We have heard that time heals all wounds,
    but right now, the wound is too deep
      for us to believe
        that it can ever be healed.
  Give us the faith and confidence we need
    to know that this aching
      will eventually be relieved,
        that, with your help,
          we will regain the ability
            to enjoy life once again.
We also ask you, Lord,
  to teach us to give comfort and support
    to one another during this trying time.
  Give each of us the ability
    to make this heartache
      a little less painful
        for all those who are feeling the loss.

Amen ✠

A Difficult Time

We have come together, Lord, to pray for (n),
    who is facing a difficult situation.
        (N) desperately needs
            your loving help,
            your care,
            your comfort,
            your support.
    We, too, will help all we can,
        but our help is limited.
(N) needs you, Lord,
    to provide the strength he[she] must have
        to face this difficulty confidently and successfully.
Dear Lord, we ask you to give (n)
    the wisdom he[she]needs
        to make the right decisions,
        to hold on to an optimistic outlook,
        to handle this problem
            without getting discouraged.
    Bless (n) with faith and peace.
We ask you, Lord, to shower your blessings on (n)
    and to let everything that's troubling him[her]
        work out for the best.

Amen ✠

An Important Decision

Lord, we come to you today to ask for your help
   in making an important decision.
   We're faced with a difficult choice
     and don't really know how to handle it.
   We all feel confused, uncertain, and incapable
     of agreeing on what's best.
Lord, we ask you to give each of us
   the wisdom,
   the patience,
   and the perseverance we need
     to face and make
       this important decision.
   Give each of us the ability
     to resolve the differences in our viewpoints,
     to examine our options with open minds,
     and to agree on a choice
       that is good and right for all of us.
We place our faith and trust in your help, Lord,
     and are open to your guidance and direction.
   We feel confident
     that if we ask
       for your loving help and guidance,
         you will lead us
           to the best possible decision.
We thank you for your help, Lord.

Amen ✠

When We Travel

We ask you, Lord, to keep us safe when we travel.
  We promise to do our part,
      to observe the rules for safety,
      to wear safety devices,
      to be responsible travelers.
  We also promise to be courteous travelers,
      to observe traveling limits and regulations,
      to be aware of the needs of fellow travelers,
      to avoid becoming hasty and impatient.
Lord, don't let us ever be guilty
  of being reckless
  or under the influence of alcohol or drugs.
  Watch over us
      so that our poor judgments
          may cause no injury
              to us or others.
Remind us, Lord, that all travel regulations
  are for our own good
      and the safety of others.
  Don't let us be tempted to do anything
      that will make travel difficult or dangerous
          for others.
Lord, we ask you to watch over us and keep us safe
  regardless of our mode of transportation:
      car, bike, bus, boat, train, plane, or foot.
  Bless our drivers, pilots, captains, and guides
      with wisdom and good judgment.
Protect us all from harm, Lord,
  and bring us safely to our destination.

Amen ✠

XIV

Special Times

Our Family's Birthday

Today is the birthday of our family.
Join us, Lord, in our celebration of this important event.
Bless each of us;
make our lives together as a family
meaningful, fulfilling, and enjoyable.
We look back upon this past year, Lord,
and thank you for all the great memories.
We thank you for all our daily shared experiences,
for all the fun we've had together,
for the troubles and squabbles we've known.
May we learn what we can from the bad times
and cherish and treasure the times that were good.
Lord, help us grow in our love for one another
and grant us the ability to make this coming year
a year that will add many new and rich experiences
to the precious storehouse of our memories.
Let it be a year filled with kindness and thoughtfulness,
Lord,
a year in which we will be ready and willing
to help one another with problems,
to forgive one another for annoyances,
to praise one another for accomplishments,
to love one another for what we are.
Dear Lord, let each member of our family
be richly blessed during this coming year
with a generous amount of health,
peace,
and happiness.

Amen ✠

A Birthday

We ask you, Lord, to bless (n).
   We're so glad that (n) is part of
      our lives.
     Thank you for the opportunity
       to share this past year with him[her].
We pray, Lord, that this coming year
   will bring (n)
     blessings of health,
     happiness,
     and a good measure of success.
   Bring (n) friends and companions
     that provide him[her]
       with generous amounts
         of warmth, comfort, fun, and love.
We ask you, Lord,
   to guide (n) throughout this year,
   to give (n)
     strength to face the challenges ahead.
   May (n) know greater faith in you
     with each passing day.
   Bless (n) with wisdom and confidence
     so that he[she] can work successfully
       toward the fulfillment
        of all his[her] dreams.
We ask, dear Lord, that you let each new year
   bring new blessings and joy to (n).

Amen ✠

Easter

Lord, we gather to celebrate
 your most splendid feast of Easter,
  to share in the joy of your Resurrection.
You suffered for us on the road to Calvary.
 You died a terrible and painful death on the cross
  so that each of us can enjoy
   an eternity of love and happiness with you.
Lord, you have shown us an overwhelming abundance
  of selfless love
  by giving your life for us.
 In return,
  we often respond to you
   by being unkind to one another,
   by being self-centered and uncaring,
    insensitive and rude.
We're sorry, Lord, for all the times we've failed
  to live up to your expectation of us.
 Let us learn to make ourselves worthy
  of the happiness you have prepared for us.
 May we do our best,
  be our best,
  give our best,
   to all of our family and friends.
Dear Lord, we thank you for allowing each of us
 to share in the joy of your Resurrection.

Amen ✠

Thanksgiving

We join hands around this table, Lord, to give you thanks.
    You have showered us with
        wonderful and bountiful blessings.
    We thank you for the opportunity
        to be together on this special day
            to share and enjoy this abundant
                and delicious feast.
    Before we eat,
        we pause for a moment
            to remember all those
                who are not surrounded
                    with abundance today.

(Pause for a moment of silence.)

We ask you, Lord, to bless and help all those who are
        lonely,
        needy,
        ill,
        desperate.
    Never let us forget
        our obligation to them.
Dear Lord, we invite you into our midst.
    Join us, celebrate with us,
        for it is your goodness and bounty that we celebrate.
We are especially grateful, Lord,
    for one another,
    for the bonds of love and loyalty
        that we share.

Amen ✠

Christmas

We thank you, Lord, for bringing us together today
    to celebrate this great holiday.
    We confess, however, that we often get so wrapped up
        in the glitz and glitter of Christmas,
            we forget what we're celebrating:
                the day you came to live among us.
You came, Lord Jesus, to teach us how to live,
    to show us how to love.
    May we always be willing and eager to learn
        as much as we can
            from all that has been written
                about your life here on earth.
    Let us learn to follow not only your teachings
        but also the wonderful example
            you set for us,
                such as love, generosity, and sacrifice.
In this season of giving, Lord,
    let us offer one another
        not only our usual Christmas gifts
            but our personal gifts as well:
                kindness,
                understanding,
                and loving concern.
Dear Lord, let us learn to share ourselves
    with one another,
        just as you have shared yourself
            and your life on earth with us.
We ask you, Lord, to give each of us
    your special Christmas blessing.

Amen ✠

Achievement

Lord, we're really proud of (n).
> We know that a lot of hard work, patience,
>> and determination
>> went into this achievement.
> We realize that nothing of value is accomplished
>> without a struggle,
>> without a firm desire to accept a challenge
>>> and see it through to its completion.

We're all very proud and happy that (n)
> was able to meet the challenge,
> accept the struggle,
> and realize success.

We thank you, Lord, for helping (n)
> and for helping all of us
>> with our accomplishments.
> Let us learn how to hold on to our dreams and
>> to work hard to achieve them.

Dear Lord, show us how to help and support one another
> in the attainment of our goals.
> Free our hearts of childish jealousies and resentments,
>> that we might rejoice with every accomplishment,
>>> seeing each as an accomplishment
>>>> for our entire family.
> Let us always be able to take great pride and real joy
>> in celebrating the accomplishments
>>> of each and every member of our family.

Amen ✠

A Special Guest

Lord, we're so happy to have (n) with us today.
  We welcome (n) into our home
    as we share our love and friendship.
  We're grateful for the pleasure of his[her] company.
We ask you, Lord, to bless (n)
  and to keep him[her] in your loving care.
We invite you, Lord, to be with us
  during this short time we have together,
    to make this visit one that will be fondly
      remembered and treasured.
As we reach out to one another and join our hands
  in a circle of love and friendship,
    we stand together in your sight, Lord,
      and ask you for your special blessing
        upon our guest
          and upon each and every one of us.
Watch over us and keep all of us safe from harm
  as we part to go our separate ways.
Grant that we may have the opportunity
  to come together in the near future
    to share this treasured friendship
      once again.

Amen ✠

The Great Outdoors

We thank you, Lord, for this chance to be together,
    to enjoy this wonderful world of yours.
    You must deeply love us
        to have provided us with a world filled
            with so many beautiful things.
We thank you, Lord, for everything:
    for the comforting warmth of the sun,
    the refreshing coolness of the breeze,
    the radiant splendor of day,
    the quiet beauty of nightfall.
We thank you for all the things that grow:
        the towering trees,
        the vast fields of grass,
        the colorful wildflowers.
We thank you for the wooded hills and rolling valleys,
    the flowing rivers and bubbling streams,
    the vast deserts and sparkling seas.
We thank you for the song of the birds,
    the whisper of the wind,
    the rhythmic sound of waves.
We thank you, Lord, for the opportunity we have today—
    and all the opportunities we have had in the past—
        to enjoy your wonderful gifts of nature.
Forgive us, Lord, for all the times
    we have taken these gifts for granted.

Amen ✷

Reunions

We come together, Lord, to celebrate and enjoy
    our kinship and friendship.
We thank you, Lord, for this opportunity
    to be with one another on this day.
    We ask you to bestow your special blessings
      upon each and every one of us.
We also invite you to join us, Lord,
    to stay in our midst,
    to share the pleasure of this event with us.
    We're blessed to be part of such a wonderful family,
      such a great and precious group of people.
    Grant that we may always love and care deeply
      for one another
        and never allow petty annoyances or jealousies
        to weaken our family bond.
    We realize that our interests,
      our opinions,
    and our viewpoints
      are often very different,
        but we rely on you
          to teach us
          to accept these differences,
          to appreciate them,
          to count them gift.
Let our understanding of one another, Lord,
    increase with each passing year,
    May our loyalty to one another
      remain forever strong.

May we remain available to one another
    to share and enjoy
        all the memories and good times.
May we continue to
    help, comfort, and support one another
        in times that are difficult.
We thank you, Lord,
    for giving each of us
        the opportunity
            to belong to this family—
            our family.

Amen ✠